2 Revere Place

DARLING MACKENZIE!
THANK YOU SO MUCH FOR YOUR
FRIENDSHIP & SUPPORT IN THIS
$ IN LIFE! HOPE YOU ENJOY THE BOOK!

2 Revere Place

poems
by Aruni N. Wijesinghe

LOVE,
Aruni

MOON
TIDE PRESS

~ 2022 ~

2 Revere Place
© Copyright 2022 Aruni N. Wijesinghe

Editor-in-chief
Eric Morago

Editor Emeritus
Michael Miller

Marketing Specialist
Ellen Webre

Proofreader
Jim Hoggatt

Front cover art
N.S. Nazir

Book design
Michael Wada

Moon Tide logo design
Abraham Gomez

2 Revere Place
is published by Moon Tide Press

Moon Tide Press
6709 Washington Ave. #9297
Whittier, CA 90608
www.moontidepress.com

FIRST EDITION

Printed in the United States of America

ISBN # 978-1-957799-01-8

Further Praise for 2 Revere Place

Aruni's debut collection is a part memoir and part coming-of-age story, crafted with tenderness, that any child of immigrants will relate to. The poet takes us from warm memories in Sri Lanka to the cold streets of New York and settles into a cul-de-sac in a traditional suburban neighborhood where a young child experiences all the joys of family and friendship as well as the many struggles common to brown kids who just want to fit in without giving up their culture. Using imagery, line breaks and other poetic elements, Aruni has given us a story that any biographer or filmmaker would wish they had created.

— Nikolai Garcia, author of *Nuclear Shadows of Palm Trees*

In *2 Revere Place*, the poet takes us on a family's journey from Sri Lanka to the United States, weaves a story heady with aromas of the Sri Lankan food from the 'home' culture, and the American food from the 'home' that the family builds in the United States. She shows us what it means to be colonized again and again, lets us feel the vertigo pull between these two 'homes.' Perhaps the most tender poems are about the father. In one poem, the child falls and the father stitches up the wound. The child says, '*I admire the tidy needlework, know that I won't come apart.* She tries *to be/like the other kids at school.* The girl lisps, and nobody can pronounce her Sri Lankan name. Yet she finally comes to the realization that [*her*] *voice is meant to be heard.* And what an important voice it is.

— Donna Spruijt-Metz

Contents

III.

IV.

VII.

Foreword

As long as there have been humans, there has been migration. For a variety of reasons, our species finds itself constantly leaving situations to which we have become accustomed in order to transplant ourselves to somewhere new. For some, migration is survival, with intolerable circumstances caused by man or God forcing us to tear ourselves away from our homes. For others, it is the desire to seek opportunities to improve our lives and the lives of those who depend on us. The luckiest are driven by curiosity, seeking new frontiers to explore in order to push the mind forward and collect new lived experiences in our relatively short lifespans.

In all these cases, the lives of both those in transit and those left behind are irrevocably transformed by the experience. Some of these stories have been documented. The vast majority, however, have been lost to time, only to be found in our generational memories.

This is why Aruni Wijesinghe, and her book that you now hold in your hands, is so important to me. I have had the honor of exploring these stories with her since we were teenagers growing up in southern California, products of the same South Asian immigrant experience in America. We bonded over these shared experiences, retreating into stories of our families, traditions, and food. At times it seemed like we were in a secret club, looking across the room at each other with a shared nod of the head and an unspoken admission that our backgrounds gave us a different take on things than others in the room.

For too long, we have accepted being misunderstood, forcing ourselves into fitting into the world around us rather than inviting them in. But as Aruni started to find her voice, I found new meaning in my life as she crafted a picture that helped me understand myself more. I am profoundly grateful that she has given a voice to so many of the feelings I have had trapped in my head.

These stories are difficult to articulate. Each answer creates new questions, forcing us to look at the world around us in new ways, ways that are sometimes diametrically opposed to the way everyone else sees it. But if my children are to appreciate how they came to be Americans, it is a story that needs to be shared, in an art form and language that is accessible to them.

Aruni's work illustrates the inflection point that separates the pre and post-immigrant experience, a bridge generation that, for a moment in time, holds both stories in their hands. My generation—which includes those who were born or raised here by immigrant parents—is the one that simultaneously understands both the trauma of displacement and the promise of the home to be.

This is a profoundly important collection of stories that need to be told. The current landscape of America didn't just come out of nowhere. It is the result of trauma, hope, resilience, growth, and interactions between different peoples. These stories find their roots in the experience of Central American migrants fleeing violence with young children in their arms. They share DNA with the Irish, Jewish, and Italian immigrants who crowded urban tenements and found themselves near the bottom of the socioeconomic ladder. They are but a shadow of the experience of newly-freed Blacks who, stripped of everything but their resilience, fought to rebuild their lives in a struggle that continues to this day.

Aruni's contribution to this corpus is just the latest chapter of the book of the American experience. I value it especially because it is also my story, but it also holds value for those of you who may be new to this particular narrative. Maybe the next time you see someone who looks like us, you will have a new appreciation of the myriad forces that shaped who we are. Maybe you will take whatever benefit you get from our interactions and confer some of your gratitude to the generations that preceded us. And maybe—just maybe—we can all move forward as one, together, as Americans.

— Shahed Amanullah, entrepreneur, former diplomat, and lifelong friend

Revere Place is where we learned to ride banana-seat bikes around the cul-de-sac. Make firefly lanterns with Hellman's mayonnaise jars. Collect juniper berries, cicada wings, maple seed pods. We would lay in the grass to watch the lawn sprinkler throw rainbows across our yard. Press clover between the pages of the phone book, for luck.

Life on that street taught us our address is a reminder to revere place, honor the life our parents built for us in a red Colonial with black shutters, the Bermuda grass lawn a soft place to fall, the porch light winking in the dusk to guide us home.

This book is dedicated to my family, and the home we created.

To Kiran, Reshan, Melia and Leila, so they can know the story before their story.

To my nangi and malli, ever my co-conspirators through childhood and beyond.

To Ammi and Thaaththi, the most intrepid people I know. Without you there would be no us.

And to Aachchi, who dreamt me a poet long before I dreamed it for myself.

I.

The Mount Lavinia Hotel, Colombo

my history begins
with the echo of betel leaves
falling on teak floorboards

shadows of wedding guests
dissolve to smoke
with push of the ballroom door

Blowfish

My poem lolls in the surf, rocked
in a cradle of mesh onion bag.
It has been swept out to sea many times,
off the beach at Trincomalee, only to return
back to the same stretch of sand.

I learn that an ancient name for the bay
is Gokarna, the *Bull's Ear*,
referring to Nandi,
guardian of Kailash,
sacred bull of Shiva.
This place, the ear of the bull,
is sacred, holiest of holies.

My poem bloats in its bag
and flies circle its mass,
waiting for something to happen.

It gestates in the bull's ear,
swelling with secrets.
Like a sack of nightmares,
spiny and menacing,
words are seeds washed up
from some deep undersea forest,
rolling in the rising tide, looking
for a place to burst open
and take root.

It is not concerned
with the depth of the harbor,
drowning deep.
It watches children race
on the wet sand, wonders
if one brave boy will break
from the pack, grab a stick of driftwood
and poke at blowfish eyes.

A group has gathered to watch
fishermen haul in an enormous net.
The sea drags men back towards the waves,
unwilling to surrender gifts

and horrors alike.

white/rice

gather sheaves by tanned armloads
hoist the weight of harvest on bent back
beat the burden of the future
against the smooth of threshing floor

pound the *wangediya*
listen to the rhythm of the pestle
as it breaches the hull
pulse of the coming meal

separate the bran from each grain
peel back the germ, render rice
less indigenous, more digestible
easier for heat to penetrate

strip away native skin
husks carried on errant wind
blow away memory of brown
leave only the tender white—

now call it polished, refined

Mangoes

I pick fruit
halfway ripe,
gift you
color change
on the kitchen counter,
blush
of hidden summer
overrunning green,
flaming the skin
with the yearning
of sweetness checked.

Jaggery

Ammi's voice answers the phone,
speaks my name
with dark sweetness of jaggery
melting in a mouth
shaped around the sound
of coming home.

Oyā kālā da
(have you eaten)

my ears are fed
with the sound of a spoon
coconut shell and teak
scraping the bottom
of the rice pot

I Carry

I am earthenware *kalaya*
balanced on fortune's hip,
brown arm nestled in groove
of the vessel's neck, brimming
with water, red dhal, betel leaves,
uncut gems, colonizer's tongue,
jungle night, Perahara lights,
pichcha mala-scented dreams.

Our parents come

with winter coats
bought from bales on the sidewalks
of Nuwara Eliya, clothing that has traveled
in the holds of ships, from America
to the port in Galle, then by truck
to the hill country, wool coats strange
against the backdrop of tea estates

with dollars sewn
into the lining of *Thaaththi's* new coat,
bills bought on the black market because
their government says that no riches
can be taken from the island,
if you go, go with nothing
but the clothes on your back

on airplanes, unlike uncles
who left the island on an ocean liner, a month
at sea, to England and not New York,
journey to colonizers' back gardens, steal
a bit of what was stolen, conquer a different island
with curried meals and a chartered engineer's acumen
for rebuilding

to New York by way
of the Netherlands, overnight in the old Amsterdam,
missing fields of tulips that wouldn't bloom
for another three months,
seeing snow fall for the first time,
learning an earlier colonizer's ways
before arriving in New Amsterdam

to JFK with no one to receive them,
no placard with our family name
printed neatly in block letters, only an address
to an apartment building in the Bronx written
in *Ammi's* tidy hand, the address they show
to the cabbie they hail outside of the airport,
snow swirling into the back door,
following the suitcases into the trunk

in a taxi, windshield wipers brush
snow from the glass, heavy flakes that fall
like scraped coconut for *pol sambol,*
Thaaththi watching the ticking meter
over the driver's shoulder, makes sure
if and when the fare hits
sixteen dollars he and *Ammi*
will pay the driver, collect their bags and walk
the remaining blocks, snow collecting
on the shoulders of second-hand winter coats
bought on the sidewalks in Nuwara Eliya,
weeks and lifetimes away

II.

Banyan

1. Characterization
> The banyan begins its life
> as a mispronunciation
> of *banniyas*, merchants who built
> a small pagoda to honor
> the shade of the fig tree. Colonizers
> later assign the colloquial name
> *strangler fig*,
> though who strangles whom is
> a question for fickle history,
> the memory of conquerors.

2. Germination
> The banyan sometimes begins life
> inside another tree, an inopportune place
> for the host. Tiny seeds, ill-suited
> for the long fall to the forest floor, fly
>
> KLM, traverse great distances,
> the luggage hold reeking of *achcharu* and
> Maldive fish, poorly packaged.
> Pips land in the crevices
> of buildings unaccustomed
> to foreign occupation.
> As the new shoots take root,
> hallways flood with spice, the air thick
> with jungle.

3. Propagation
> Aerial roots grope for ground,
> coil to join the trunk. Old trees spread
> laterally, every shoot connecting
> to the parent, creating an illusion grove.
> *They all seem to be related, don't they?*
> the neighbors say. The native species are
> crowded out. The old forest flees.
> New trees take root.

4. Population

> At times the host is lost
> in a web of invading roots,
> the corner bodega supplanted with
> an India Cash and Carry.
> The banyan maintains the hollow,
> creates a sheltering place.
> A new colony
> can thrive in this vacuum,
> find grocery stores and temples nearby.

5. Proliferation

> Breaking open a fig reveals
> a tender, hidden flower.
> Fragrance lures wasps
> into a surrogate womb,
> home to the future swarm.

> Wasps who invade female fruit
> seek to fumble the secret flower,
> seduced by an unknown perfume.
> Wasps who enter
> the male fruit lay eggs, plant
> new ideas. The spent wasps collapse
> in their houses of flesh,
> die surrounded by sweetness.

Locals

Every day that January, *Ammi* and *Thaaththi*
bundle up in second-hand coats,
walk the few blocks
from 1770 Grand Concourse to their jobs
at an inner-city hospital.

The first earnings they save are for two tickets
back to Sri Lanka. New Yorkers and their winters
are too frigid for a young couple accustomed
to warmth of curries and equatorial suns. Dr. Fried,
a radiologist at Bronx-Lebanon, tells them
*Don't judge Americans by New Yorkers. When
the weather warms, so will the people.*

They try roasted chestnuts from cart vendors,
. wait for the eventual thaw.

In the spring they decide to spend
the money they've saved on a new car.
Two thousand three hundred dollars cash buys
a 1969 Volkswagon Beetle, Montana Red,
and road enough to reveal a new continent.

One warm day they visit Battery Park, take photos
of one another, the Statue of Liberty poised
in the background, accept that they are

locals, not tourists.

November, 1969

The first November
Ammi and *Thaaththi* spend in the Bronx
Ammi is nine months pregnant.
They know nothing of pilgrims
and Plymouth Rock, haven't tasted
turkey and cranberry sauce, don't have
a long dinner table of guests.

Uncle Arnold brings
lechón and *arroz con gandules*
prepared by his wife, Maria.
It's not a textbook holiday meal,
but it's warm and lovingly prepared.
Two days later, *Ammi* goes into labor.
I am born on Sunday morning,
the first American in my family.

That first Thanksgiving,
Ammi and *Thaaththi* learn
the best of America
from strangers who embrace us
in their Jewish-Puerto Rican fold,
make us their own.

At First Sight

My hands, two beached starfish,
push back the flash of *Thaaththi's* camera.
Aachchi holds me for the first time
the day after she arrives from Sri Lanka,
four days after my birth.

My eyes large. Her eyes shrink
when she smiles down at me. Tiny,
I squirm in her lap.

Her hands, used to cupping something
fragile, know how to hold a new life, connect
the thread of generations continents apart.

Curtains behind us gold-flowered,
brown fabric chair matching a non-descript sofa.
Hospital-furnished apartment
still foreign to us.
These walls hold a universe,
wet-glistening.

Thaaththi's camera flutters
its all-seeing eye, captures
this love at first sight.

At the 174-175th Street Subway Station, Bronx

one hand tucks into *Aachchi's* coat pocket,
the other clutches the sun yellow
of a packet of Chiclets Chewing Gum.
I am allowed one piece of gum, making space
to turn the box into a lone maraca,
the white pieces clicking
like blank mah-jongg tiles.

The wind of passing trains
makes her nylon sari billow
under a tweedy winter coat, but
the square toes of her brown shoes
root steady on the platform.

Sweet Teeth

On weekends we go to Woolworth's on Fordham
to feed our eyes. My favorite part
of the store is the candy aisle.
I shake purple boxes
of Good N' Plenty, listen to the click
of Chiclets in cellophane-wrapped yellow.
The best are the blue tin cans
of Charms Sour Balls. I cannot wait
to get back to the apartment,
beg *Thaaththi* to peel back the tin lid,
peer into a universe of small planets
tumbled in one sugary mass.

On the Square

We shop at S. Klein on the Square,
known for honest and fair deals
on the square.
We head upstairs to the bins,
discounted clothes heaped high,
so many grasping hands rummaging.
If a shirt doesn't fit, *Aachchi* can
take it in, hem it, make it work.

After our bargain hunting,
Ammi and *Thaaththi* buy
two Nathan's hot dogs,
heap the steaming buns with mounds
of free sauerkraut. It's cheaper
than buying each of them a second dog.
They make it work.

Engagement Party

Aunty Rani is nurse at Bronx-Lebanon
with *Ammi* and *Thaaththi*, another foreigner
recruited by the hospital. When her marriage
to a physician in India is arranged, she hosts a party
to celebrate her engagement. She pins a snapshot
of the groom who becomes our Uncle Rana
to the shoulder of her sari
where the jeweled pallu falls away.

She leaves New York a bride and returns
a new wife. Her wedding bangles tinkle
with each gesture, the sindoor in her hair
vivid as blood.

The rhythm of their family pulses in the hallways,
perfume of cumin and coriander seeping
from under the door. Like *Ammi* and *Thaaththi*,
they add American children to the nation
and add South Asian values to the children
so that we all hold two countries.

Eventually they move to Abilene, Texas,
become Kodak snapshots
tucked into yearly holiday cards.

But on the night of the engagement party,
she is beautiful Aunty Rani, laughing, full of hope
for the future she will fly to India to meet.

Bedtime Story

At three years old I refuse to sleep
until one of my parents reads me
Goldilocks and the Three Bears.
This is our nightly ritual. I never ask
for a different story. I insist on drifting
to sleep with the minutiae of the porridge,
the chairs, and the tiniest bed
swirling in my mind.

If my weary parents try to rush
my bedtime ritual by skipping over details,
I wake up and correct them. *No, Thaaththi,
first she sits in the Papa Bear's chair. No Ammi,
you forgot to say that Baby Bear's porridge
was just right.* I do not abide any shortchanging
of my nightly bowlful of Goldilocks
and her forest escapades.

My parents are perplexed at why this tale
of a small blonde on a crime spree
has captured my imagination.

Crocuses

My *aachchi* buys me
six crocus bulbs at Woolworth's,
potted in a bright green container
shaped like a wooden clog.
My parents explain
that soon I will have
cup-shaped flowers,
that in Holland
there are fields
of purple stretching
to the horizon. I carry
my buried promises
to the balcony
where the weak city sun
can awaken my slumbering stars.

But my three-year-old soul
is not blessed
with patience, and the roots
branching below the soil
are so enticing. Every day
I yank my crocuses
out of their container, stare
at these things more onion
than flower. Eventually they wither
on a windowsill, exhausted
from the effort of clinging,
desperate for their handful of earth.

In Praise of Urban Romance

The two of them—like any other pair
sharing a brownstone, second-floor walk-up—
lean out the window, wave to strangers
water the flower boxes on the sill.

They walk to the corner market, repair shop
invite the neighbors over for dinner,
tell corny jokes, give each other ill-fated
haircuts, collect bottle caps, paper clips.

They argue and make up, shrug off the spats
grow in their idiosyncrasies, laugh
those rambling conversations at bath time
small moments of awkward intimacy.

On Sesame Street, love wears striped sweaters—
uncomplicated, just as life could be.

Precious Enough

The Formans are the first friends
Ammi and *Thaaththi* make in America.
I grow up calling the parents
Uncle Arnold and Aunty Maria,
their five children my older cousins.
Our adoptive family attends every birthday party
in our apartment on Grand Concourse,
and *Thaaththi* captures
patent leather, corduroy,
pigtails and knee socks
on Ektachrome color slides.

One year they gift me a necklace,
the five letters of my name
suspended from a delicate chain.

Uncle Arnold and Aunty Maria know
I will spend years searching card stores
and souvenir shops for something –
anything – with my name on it.
I will waste hours wishing
for personalized key tags and coffee mugs.
I will squander countless moments
on jealously of the Michelles and Stephanies
in my classes, dream
of average, commonplace.

This fragile talisman rests
against my collarbone, reminds me
my name is precious enough
for gold.

Her Hands

for Constance Rachel Wijesinghe, my paternal Aachchi, who we called Colomba Aachchi

learned skills of sewing, tatting, crochet
feminine accomplishments
of a colonial age

wore the engagement ring
passed down to me on my wedding day
sapphire winking like the sea off Galle Face

wrote lessons on chalkboards
assigned homework, corrected exams,
wrote words of encouragement

composed lines of poetry
words dripping from the nibs of fountain pens
forget-me-not

soothed small children
laid damp cloths on troubled foreheads
my aunty, my uncle, my father

prepared *kukulmas curry* and *kiri hodi*
in the kitchen of a small New York City apartment
heirloom meals cooked for us

slipped us
clandestine rolls of cherry Life Savers
fished from the bottom of her black pocketbook

hands that touched our lives
in the same gentle manner
of her voice, her smile, her laughing eyes

reborn as birds
soaring above clamor of the city, sailing over oceans
circling rice paddies in her native Ceylon

home to roost, to wait for us

Island Fauna

When I am two-and-a-half
and on my first trip to Sri Lanka,
my cousin Shian and I become fast friends.
He carries me everywhere,
points out animals to me,
explains everything we see.

In Aunty Madonna and Uncle Edgar's garden
there is a line of ants busy around the base of a palm,
swarming a fallen coconut.
I ask Shian what they are.
They are ants, he tells me.
Have you not seen them before?
I ask to be set down, squat in the grass,
watch the industry between the shards
of exploded fruit. *I don't think we have these
at the Bronx Zoo,* I tell him.

He laughs and crouches in the grass with me,
his shadow protecting me
from an unforgiving sun.

we slip on a dark skin of words

incarnate histories
bridge continents
climb the stairs
of high-rise apartment buildings

leave the clamor of America on the doormat
remove our shoes, walk gentle into the house
build a home enough
for ancestors and children
to sit together

pass the rice and dhal,
eat with turmeric-stained fingertips,
smell of cardamom clinging to our hair

we mingle English and Sinhala
our open mouths bold enough to eat
two worlds at once

Thaaththi's eyes are closed in family albums,

his split-second timing lowering his lids
the moment the flash bulb fires.
Thaaththi's smile, caught mid-laugh,
is wide and gap-toothed like mine,
and he always smiles full-mouthed.

Usually he is behind the camera,
peering through the view-finder, composing
memory inside the studio of his Nikon.
He poses us in front of birthday cakes
and national monuments. We squint and complain,
blinded by the sun.

Thaaththi closes his eyes in photos,
imagines our futures. He picks us up
from the Fotomat, protects us under plastic
on new pages, guards us against harsh light
that might fade our history.

III.

Magic Mirror, or What Did Childhood Teach You About Visibility

I watched Romper Room
every day.

      Miss Nancy peered through her Magic Mirror,

                    never saw me,
                    never said my
                    name.

Barbie Coloring Book, or How I Learn What Is Beautiful

Today I show Mary Alice Maneri
my new Barbie wristwatch. She compliments
the beauty of the sky-colored band, asks me
the time so I can practice. She finds
a coloring book with a portrait of Barbie looking
just like she does on the face of my watch.

Mary Alice is good at coloring.
She is older, maybe in junior high already, but
she still makes time for me.

Mary Alice stays inside the lines. She knows
how to glide crayons gently. She chooses
pink for Barbie's lips, the color
of Jackson and Perkins rosebuds
from *Ammi's* garden. She uses an orange crayon
with a light touch for Barbie's creamy skin.
I hand her yellow for Barbie's blonde flip hairstyle,
light blue for her wide headband.

When Barbie is complete, Mary Alice tears
the page from the book, prints both of our names
across the bottom. Three names: *Mary Alice, Aruni*
and *Barbie*. I carry the page carefully
back to my house, affix it to the refrigerator.
I look at Barbie every day. I carry her face
on my small wrist where she counts down
the hours until I am big.

But my hair stays black and straight
and I have to use a brown crayon
never quite the right shade. I am always
outside the lines, my pictures never
Barbie perfect.

Philip, or What Do You Know of the Gentleness of Boys

When I fall off my bike in front of his house
he carries me the whole block
                             back home.

With a fingertip, he brushes welling tears,
tells me he has never seen eyes
                             so big.

He blows on my ragged palms,
makes me forget
                      the sting.

Easy Bake Oven

The determination
of a six-year-old child:

patience to bake
a three-and-one-half inch cake

on the heat of a 100-watt
incandescent lightbulb,

retinas seared from staring
into the miniature oven window,

after-image of tiny suns
dancing across closed eyelids.

Playing Hooky

I curl under a juniper bush,
collecting dusty purple berries
in my cupped palm.
A Nancy Drew book lies
face down on the grass, yellow spine
bright against the cool lawn.

I should be practicing scales
from a Czerny exercise book,
cream pages calling faintly
from the Baldwin upright piano.
But this afternoon, the sun gilds the world
pollen. I gather fistfuls of fairy pearls,
my hands smelling of early gin and escape.

Volante Pizza

is between Waldbaum's Supermarket
and Tip-Top Stationers. Young men
in white t-shirts, sleeves rolled above
biceps, work the counter. We watch them
answer phones, slide slices
in and out of the hot oven
with a big metal pizza peel, dispense
Cokes into waxed paper cups, spindle
the order checks on a metal spike.

Our favorite thing is to watch them toss
pizzas. They knead with the heels
of calloused hands, the slap of dough
a counterpoint to music floating
out a battered transistor radio. Crusts hover
in perfect circles before collapsing
back to outstretched hands, a syncopated
choreography of flour, yeast, water
and timing.

We watch from the sidewalk,
chewing our Bubble Yum and blowing
pink bubbles that collapse
across our sweaty noses. We think these men
are brothers, like the Flying Wallendas.
We assign them names. Anthony Volante.
Michael Volante. Maybe the handsomest
is named Dino. We watch them send
pie after pie sailing. We wonder
if they have an act, if they perform
in front of adoring fans, throwing dough
instead of knives under a big top
somewhere in Nyack or Pearl River.

Years later, in a language class at UCLA,
I learn *volante* is the Italian word
for flying. Maybe Tony, Mikey and Dino
escaped Volante Pizza, left dough tangled
in the blades of the ceiling fan, flew far
from Rockland county to find their own fame
away from the oven, away from childhood,
away from us.

ac•ro•pho•bi•a

Every four-week swim session
at the South Orangetown Middle School pool
ends with a jump from the high dive.

I have mastered flutter kicks, hold my breath
under water for an eternity, dead man's float
as well as any corpse. But I know the ladder
up to the diving board leads to calamity.

For two summers I have climbed the stairway
of dread, knees knocking. Inched my way
to the edge of the plank, miles above
the algal green. The swim teacher,
hair sea-lion slick, treads water far below.
She holds her arms out, promises
to catch me. I stall at the end of the diving board,
bladder bursting. My suction-cup toes refuse
to detach me from my bobbing perch. I balk.
Crawl back to the ladder. Force a line
of frustrated swimmers to descend. Slink
my way to the locker room.

By the third summer my cowardice is legend.
On the last day of class I join the queue of swimmers.
I tug at the seat of my bathing suit. Shiver
in my chlorinated puddle. Wait my turn for death.
I follow a pair of pruny heels up metal stairs,
focus on two wrinkled soles ascending ahead of me.
Try not to notice bodies plummeting. Shrieks echoing.

I edge my way to the end of the board. Peer into the abyss.
Snickering gives way to chants of *Jump! Jump!*
Jump! When I look over my shoulder, faces crowd
the top of the ladder. *Jump!* reverberates off the tiled walls.
I screw my eyes shut and step out into nothingness—

am borne aloft on updraft. I sail over the pool,
skim lane lines with my wings, circle
aluminum bleachers full of parents waiting
for their damp children. I escape, fly
through an open transom window into the bright.

An American Sonnet of Familial Designations

One week when I am eight years old I call
my parents Mom and Dad. I try to be
like other kids at school. I practice terms
they print on cards for Mother's Day, rehearse

the names they shout from down the block at dusk.
I try on words like shirts that don't quite fit,
the shoulders tight, the sleeves too short. I bend
my tongue around new vowels I never use,

the sounds too low, my lips un-shaped. I find
three letters scant, my love too broad to cup
in words so short. My *Thaaththi* and *Ammi* are
too big to be contained in Dad and Mom. I leave

American ideas of dear to those
with narrow mouths who live on other streets.

Denville, NJ

Ceylon Association summer picnics
fathers in shirt sleeves, mothers in denim skirts
aunties set out foil pans of short eats
we sit in the grass, eat lamprais with our fingers

before the cricket game begins, voices join
for a different national anthem,
Namo, Namo Matha! soaring into the blue, sung
with damp eyes and sighs in the throat

at Uncle Jay and Aunty Therese's house
Shamil teaches us to play carrom, how to dust
the wooden board with talcum,
make the coins ricochet off wooden bumpers

Chinese checkers on the family room rug
Lakmini in her white dress and matching tights
cousins listen to parents call one another
akka and *malli*, imagine them as children

when we get ready to leave, Shamil stoops
to touch *Thaaththi's* feet, calls him *Baappa,*
bāla Aappa, younger father, and we see
our father as more than just ours

laughter drifts out to the front yard
eat mulberries straight from the vines
our mouths stained late-summer violet
crickets sing in the dusk, bid us safe journey

Aunty Rani gifts *Ammi* a sari,

a ripple of teal and emerald chiffon undulating
off the coast at Trincomalee, embroidered
with fine gold thread and sprayed with sequins
the size of masoor dhal. Silk shimmers like sun
glinting off the sea that ebbs between Sri Lanka
and India, like laughter between women, knowing
and bright. *Ammi* floats in a silken blur at parties draped
in Aunty Rani's gift, her high-heeled sandals peeping
from beneath the pleats when she dances *baila*
with *Thaaththi*. The tear where her heel caught
during a turn around the basement dance floor
is hastily mended with a bit of bias tape because
nothing can interrupt her joy. The flaw makes the sari
more beautiful, a ribbon of grace *Ammi* trails
across firefly-lit nights at 2 Revere Place, the pallu
a victory flag, the shed of sequins leading
back to blue-green tide lapping a beach in Lanka.

Glow

The summer I am seven years old
Philip Maneri from down the street
teaches me
to catch fireflies
in empty Hellman's jars,
air holes punched in the tin lids.
We light our library books
with flickering lanterns,
and beating wings cast
tiny shadows on words.
We release our miniature lamps,
glints of lightning
in our cupped hands,
and return to lives
behind screen doors.

That same summer
Geoffrey Maneri shows me
fireflies still glow
after he kills them.
His sneakers smear
comet tails across our porch.
He smashes the bugs
between sweaty palms, anointing
his face and arms
in their bioluminescent deaths—
reminding me boys can paint themselves
with the glow
of what they destroy.

I am a late-blooming bike rider

purple Schwinn
with handlebar streamers
and white wicker basket
punctuated with plastic daisies
in pink, yellow, blue

Ammi and *Thaaththi* take turns
running in endless circles
holding onto the back
of the banana seat
hundreds of loops
around the cul-de-sac

scrape of training wheels
against the asphalt of Revere Place
as I struggle for balance
a steady hand on the frame
keeps me from the fall

Joining Seams

I don't see the garden stake
buried in the tomato bush,
slim green tendrils winding
around hidden support.
The fruits are slow to emerge
the summer I am seven,
young legs not long enough, my jump
too shallow to clear the plant.

Pain snakes up my spine
when the stake breaks
skin. The slow welling of red
leaves me wild-eyed. I stumble,
my Keds kicking up clods of dirt. I scramble
towards the sliding glass door, leave
a blood trail across the wooden decking.

Thaaththi whisks me into the house,
sets me down on the Formica counter.
His large hands steady me and he keeps me
distracted with a stream of questions:
how did this happen, why was I jumping,
where is the stick? I trace the sparkles
on the countertop, my hiccups subside.
He holds a tissue to my nose, then
leaves to retrieve his black briefcase.

He says that I need stitches
but not a trip to the hospital in the Bronx
where he works. His hands lift
supplies out of the briefcase: Betadine swabs,
gauze squares, Lidocaine in an hourglass vial,
a disposable syringe. At last, he pulls out
a sterile suture kit,
needle curved like the moon,
threaded with a sky-blue nylon thread.

He transforms our 1970s kitchen
into a makeshift operating room.
Paper towels drape the wound area,
penlight clasped between his lips illuminates
the surgical field. Betadine is cold on my leg.
I clench my eyes shut
at the *tap-tap-tap* of his fingernail
against the vial, then the snap
of glass breaking. I focus on
the hum of fluorescent lights overhead.

He joins the edges
of my gash, piecing me whole.
The tug of the nylon tethers me
to a surgeon with a father's face.
The blue thread is startling
against my skin. He covers my stitches
with two Band-Aids in the shape of an *x*.
There might be a scar, he says,
but you are okay. He sets me back down
on the linoleum floor, kisses my forehead
and nudges me towards the door.
He turns his back to clear
surgical detritus from the counter.

I go back outside and sit on the wooden deck.
I lift the edges of the bandage,
admire the tidy needlework,
know that I won't come apart.

Left out in the field,

I use the pocket of my glove
more to gather clover than to scoop up grounders.
Left field seems the safest place to put me, the worst
player in the Tappan Zee Girls' Softball League.
I never learn to swing a bat with my eyes
open, and I only get on base when I'm walked,
my walk more apology than hustle.
They position me where likely
I won't have to field any stray balls.
I don't mind.

Alone in my room, I watch the Yankees
win the pennant in 1978. My team
is also the Yankees, the Tappan Yankees,
and not the Bronx Bombers. We come in second
despite me. Still, I bask in reflected fame.

I trade baseball cards
with the kids at the bus stop. I keep Bucky Dent
on my nightstand. He and I have two things in common:
people call us *Indian*, and they don't expect
much from us on the diamond.

Miss Yvonne

always writes in pencil,
the scratch of graphite on pages
of sheet music. She notes
the measures I should practice,
jots *staccato* and *legato*
in the margins. If the mood changes
she rubs out old rules, replaces them
with charms meant to turn me
into a piano prodigy. I want to hear
Minuet in G Major in my head,
but Bach drowns, his music
corrected by the furious scrabble
of Miss Yvonne's pencil.

Listen in Sinhala, Answer in English

Receptive bilingualism:

A passive speaker (also referred to as a receptive bilingual or passive bilingual) is a category of speaker who has had enough exposure to a language in childhood to have a native-like comprehension of it, but has little or no active command of it.

In the mid-1970s, *Punchi Maama*
and *Ranji Nanda* immigrate to America
with our two cousins and their *aachchi*.
They stay with us in Tappan for a couple of weeks,
all of us together in an extended tribe,
two new playmates under our roof.

Our cousins can communicate
in Sinhala, a language I understand
but cannot speak. This is their superpower.
They whisper secrets in a code
I long to break.

I know the words
for hungry, sleepy, the names
of my favorite dishes.
But when I try to speak, syllables snag
on my teeth, wind around my American tongue,
leave me blushing-mute.

Outside of the house I have no one
to practice Sinhala with. It is enough
that I have to explain why I don't call my parents
Mom and Dad, let alone correct
my mispronounced name. Every day
my ears overflow with words,
my throat choked
with all I cannot say.

Magicicada Septemdecim

The summer of 1979 is the season
of the seventeen-year cicadas,
every day humming
with bug love songs.
We ride our shiny bikes
around the cul-de-sac
looking for wings.

Our town is littered
with discarded husks,
and every kid on Revere Place
an entomologist
hungry for wings.
We collect them
in plastic sandwich bags
and empty mint tins.
We sift through sand in the gutters
and look for what is left behind
by transient swarms.

I don't know about the plagues of Egypt
(though those are locusts). At home
we are Buddhists, so I don't learn
the reference until much later.
I busy myself hoarding insect sails,
unaware of any possible portent.
I hold one up as a tiny monocle
and look back at my house
through its lens, organza frail.

Summer Salt

we are another American family
fleeing the suburbs in a packed station wagon
spend a week of our summer on the Jersey Shore
rent a condominium a few blocks from the beach

fleeing the suburbs in a packed station wagon
we crave sunshine, sandcastles, waves licking our toes
rent a condominium a few blocks from the beach
neighbors ride bikes back from the shore in the twilight

we crave sunshine, sandcastles, waves licking our toes
we buy saltwater taffy from boardwalk hawkers
neighbors ride bikes back from the shore in the twilight
while parents drink piña coladas at sunset

we buy saltwater taffy from boardwalk hawkers
eat Nathan's hot dogs and French fries from paper cups
while parents drink piña coladas at sunset
the Ferris wheel spins us through a candy floss sky

eat Nathan's hot dogs and French fries from paper cups
spend a week of our summer on the Jersey Shore
the Ferris wheel spins us through a candy floss sky
we are another American family

We are another American family.

Watering

When we move to Tappan,
Ammi and *Thaaththi* plant
fifty-seven different varieties
of Jackson and Perkins roses
around half the perimeter of 2 Revere Place.
They buy some bushes at the local nursery,
order others from the annual catalog.

Every week *Ammi* waters each bush by hand,
holds the brass nozzle at the end
of fifty feet of Cayman green garden hose
like the head of a cobra. Her other hand clutches
the curved handle of a black nylon umbrella
to shade herself from the midday sun.

The neighbor lady leans over the white fence
to chat. She looks quizzically at the umbrella,
rubs baby oil on her freckled shoulders.
She adjusts her oversized sunglasses, shrugs.
Ammi continues with her watering,
knows this woman has never seen

sadhus in saffron robes
walking between paddy fields,
a wavering line of flames amid the green,
each carrying a black umbrella
to shield himself from the tropical sun.

She maintains her smooth skin all her life,
understands that, unlike roses,
some beauty thrives in the shade.

Rockland County Canticle

detonation of crabapple tree
frothing pink, shooting stars the length
of each branch, profusion of lovely

ticking sprinkler head
counting down the morning
parse each flung rainbow

whisper drift of dandelion down
caught on the updraft
this first inhalation of summer

intoned suburban mantra
of lawnmower blades, counterpoint
strum of garden rake across Bermuda blue

trill of tomatoes still swelling
the vine, bursting seeds
impatient with waiting

squeak of swing set chains
bottoms of our sneakers leave
footprints on the clouds

drip of Jell-O popsicles overflowing
Dixie cups, trickle down forearms
sugar stains blooming our bare knees

squawk of crow struggling
in the jaws of our orange tabby
breaks free, spirals into the blue

murmur pussywillow velvet,
brush across lips pursed
soft, kitten dreaming

humming cicadas fill the dusk
violin string pulse of life
mating calls herald a distant dawn

sigh the screen door hinges
soft clicks of latches
shut the hymnals, close the night

IV.

Born thirsty for language,

I learn to eavesdrop early,
sit quietly on the edge of life
and drink words. I discover
all things have two names.
Milk and *kiri.*
                    Rice and *bāth.*
                              Baby and *babā.*

Even I have two names.

                         There is the name
that folds me in hand-loomed comfort,
every syllable crooned. Then
there is the name that people trip
over at school, vowels elongated,
stresses misplaced. It is unthinkable
not to respond when the teacher calls me
my un-name, so I divide myself in two.

There is the home-me who removes
my shoes when I enter the house, eats
rice and dhal with my fingers, recites
stanzas in Pali at bedtime so
the Noble Triple Gem will bless me.

                         Then there is
the school-me who wears Keds
that squeak against the linoleum, carries
baloney sandwiches, foil-wrapped Ding Dongs
and milk money in a Snoopy lunchbox, recites
the Pledge of Allegiance

so that a God
              who doesn't know my name
will bless the country
                    that is home
                              to both of me.

Crayola Colors of the World Crayons, 24 Count Assorted Colors, Child

(as listed on Walmart.com, June 2021)

in 1974, first grade
not a single crayon
in the 64-count box
the right shade –
Brick, Brown, Burnt Orange,
Burnt Sienna, Chestnut, Mahogany,
Peach, Salmon, Sepia or Tan –
my self-portraits
never fridge-worthy

one dollar and thirty-seven cents
at the La Habra Walmart
could have resolved
so many questions
during art class
at William O. Shaefer Elementary

lower case "a"

I learn to print my name
in English, starting
with the capital letter "A,"
steady ladder, pitched
like the roof of our house
at 2 Revere Place.

But I want to start my name
with the small "a", its arm
curled over a bowed head,
Kandyan dancer's pose, shaped
like the Sinhala *ayanna*,
the self I grow into.

Oreos, or How We Learn Compliance

Mrs. Mahonic, our kindergarten teacher,
says that she has Oreos coming out her ears.

Every day of the week a classmate is assigned
to bring a package of cookies to share
for snack break. At the end of every month
Mrs. Mahonic sends home a mimeographed calendar
with the cookie assignments so that our parents
know when it's our turn.

We rotate being daily milk monitors, pairs
rolling the wooden wheelbarrow down the halls
to the cafeteria to pick up half-pint cartons.
We are discouraged from blowing bubbles
in our milk. Mrs. Mahonic does not enjoy
wiping up cloudy lava flows from the tabletops.

Almost everyone brings a package of Oreos
even though Mrs. Mahonic is weary of our smiles
caked in black volcanic crumbs, or worse,
cookies abandoned after we excavate
the creamy filling.

We all know that Oreos are the safest choice.
No one wants to be *that kid*
who brings off-brand cookies, or worse,
Saltines or cream crackers, because Mom forgot
to add Oreos to the list she takes to the A & P.
The last thing you do in kindergarten is
call attention to yourself for bringing
the wrong snacks.

Next Year's Marigolds

Before we dig up the withered plants
at the end of summer, *Aachchi*
will break off the last dried blooms,
her hands methodical as she separates
blossoms from their stems.
In the spring she will sprinkle
tiny matchsticks of orange and yellow
in the fallow soil.

But for now, *Nangi*, *Malli* and I plant marigolds
in the beds on either side of the sloped driveway,
sprinkling seeds from envelopes
printed with drawings of imminent buds.
Pom-poms flame in the waning summer,
illuminate the path we wheel our bikes
at the end of each day.

As Indian summer gives way
to autumn, the flowers dry.
Faded blossoms turn brown and papery,
rustle as we walk home from the bus stop.
Aachchi deadheads the plants, catches
dying petals and stamen in a blue aerogram
stamped from Sri Lanka.
She tucks the future into a kitchen drawer,
guards it until next spring
when she will turn the earth gently,
let the past fall from her fingertips,
seed a new year.

If Judy Blume Was My Aunt

Her name would be
my middle name
instead of a Sanskrit word
for a flower that doesn't grow
in New York City.

At family parties
I would sit with her
while she'd sneak Virginia Slims.
We'd skip the rice and curry, steal away
to McDonald's for burgers and Cokes.

I'd finally have
the life I checked out
of the school library,
the simplicity of meatloaf dinners
and Shawn Cassidy records.

She'd give me
a soft-focus adolescence
and the reassurance that I would
eventually bud, my body flowering
on its own mysterious schedule.

She'd gift me a diary,
tell me to start with lists
of boys' names, streets, colors:
Andrew Mallon, the two Aldo Leones,
Revere Place, Howard Avenue, Lester Drive,
dogwood pink—

these lists would become my answers.

1977

Childhood
is
a broken swing.

Aachchi Interprets American Food, a List

tuna sandwiches
made without mayonnaise
on toasted white bread,
then wrapped in aluminum foil

we never get peanut butter and jelly,
this foreign combination of sweet deemed
not nutritious

hot dogs, cold
folded in a piece of toast,
ketchup squirted in a handmade foil packet

milk money
wrapped in a piece of foil
so that we won't lose dimes
in the bottoms of lunch sacks or corduroy pockets

doughnuts
made from canned biscuit dough
stamped out with lids from Hellman's mayonnaise jar
cap from a sauce bottle to cut out the holes,
fried in a blackened *thachchi*
and dusted with granulated sugar

pizza
crust made with Bisquick
topped with Ragú spaghetti sauce
Kraft American Singles
and chopped hot dogs

fried wontons
stuffed with Libby's canned corn beef
sautéed with onions,
served at parties alongside *vadai* and *patties*,
paper doilies absorbing the grease

Scotch eggs
that we call egg cutlets
and grow up thinking are
a Sri Lankan dish, never realize
they are legacy of colonization

Buttercups, or what we learn of falling in love is not from boys

girls who sit on the school lawn
plucking buttercups
from between the blades
of red fescue, who hold blooms
underneath one another's chins,
who believe that a yellow glow
means an affinity for butter

and don't realize
reflected gold is a code of love
between girls, who don't yet know
to still blossoming hearts, too young
to understand this flush
will be redirected to boys
who will uproot us
and trample small signs
of our burgeoning Spring

so we abandon our gold
in the field where we found it,
return to the classroom to sit at desks
row upon row, bled of color

Dear God,

I don't think you know me
as I am Buddhist and you are not,
but I seem to talk to you every day
at school, during the Pledge,
my hand on my heart.

If we are one nation under You,
indivisible, why do I feel split
into two people?

And does the half of me
that asks you to bless America,
you know, in the song,
have Your ear?

Hopscotch
after Saddiq Dzukogi

I take a piece of chalk
and draw out a grid
on the edge
of the schoolyard.
I mark lines
carefully, outline a runway
where I can land.

I number
each square,
some
in
a
column,
some
side by each
to plant both sneakers
before the next leap.

I throw a stone
to mark
my unsteady journey

before I spin around
for the bounding return.

Every day I am born
an acrobat balancing
on one foot:

boarding the school bus,
eating bologna sandwiches
answering to my name mispronounced.

Then back to hopping
on my South Asian foot,
eating rice for dinner,
calling my parents *Ammi* and *Thaaththi*,
not Mom and Dad,

removing my shoes inside our house
so I don't track in the chalk
of leaping between two worlds

I Hate Kickball

I hate the sickening thud
of sneakers against the red
that is never sufficiently inflated
for the game. The *thwack* of shoe
against rubber sounds like kicking
a swollen corpse fished out of a river.

I hate that the "pitch" feels like bowling for kids
and I am the front pin.
I hate the vibrating bounce
coming towards me at home plate.
I hate the teacher's advice to keep my eyes
open when I attempt to kick the ball
away from me.

I hate the *zip-zip* of corduroy legs
as I try to run to first base. I hate the dust
that collects in the cuffs of my pants.

I hate the shouting, the calls of
let's see some hustle out there.

I hate everyone else having fun
when I just want to go back inside
and read.

Lisp

Every other Thursday afternoon
the year I am in third grade
at William O. Shaefer Elementary
I go to speech therapy
to have my lisp corrected.

We report to a small cinderblock room
no bigger than a broom closet
across the hall from the library.
Wendy, Andrew Mallon and I meet
with the school speech therapist. She is
a middle-aged woman with thick calves
and perfect elocution. We spend forty minutes
reciting words full of serpentine sounds,
brows knitted above pursed child-mouths.
A soft susurration accompanies the sound
of rubber-soled Keds squeaking
against industrial linoleum.

Brightly colored placards glare down at us,
cartoon mouths grimacing. Paper faces
illustrate the proper shape of vowels,
bite of bits of consonants.

The therapist wills my unruly tongue to repent,
coaxes unwilling s's from behind
bared baby teeth.

She never realizes
she has been mispronouncing my name
since the beginning of the school year;
elongating vowels, misplacing accents,
anglifying the music of my ancient Sanskrit name.

I am too ashamed to correct her.

Goldie Unlocks

after Ron Koertge

She rattled the doorknob, then let herself in.
She called it taking shelter.
She didn't think of it as it breaking and entering.

She sampled all three bowls of porridge, dipping her spoon
repeatedly.
She complained about the first two. She wolfed down the third.
She didn't think of it as petty theft.

She sat in all three chairs, fidgeting.
She dented the cushions, scuffed the legs. She broke the third.
She didn't think of it as destruction of property.

She climbed the steps to the bedroom, each stair creaking.
She rumpled the sheets, left smudges with her dirty shoes.
She slept in the smallest bed, undisturbed by conscience.

She screamed when she saw bears, didn't try to defend her actions.
She brushed past the bewildered three, taking the stairs two at a time.
She never thought of it as trespassing.

She knew her golden curls were her passport to the world.
She never doubted her right to be anywhere, do anything,

every door unlocked.

4711

Every childhood fever summons
Aachchi's bottle of 4711
(known to us as *OH-dee-coh-lone*)
and a worn handkerchief.

Eau de cologne is the panacea
for every ill. Headache to nightmare,
bump to bruise, every pain
wiped away with a swipe
of *Aachchi's* hanky.
Nangi, *Malli* and I connect the tang
of cologne with delirium
and the waking from it,
the turquoise and gold label
a charm against catastrophe.
Danger evaporates
when *Aachchi* lays damp cloth
across our skins, spiriting malady
from our limbs, restoring health.
Our resilience is perfumed
with *aqua mirabilis*.

A gin martini evokes
the glass bottle on the nightstand,
two weeks of chicken pox,
and *Aachchi's* fragrant hands
lifting me from disaster.

Octobering

Toughskin jeans that lasted the schoolyear,
impractical suede shoes,
and a pale buckskin jacket
embroidered with flowers
and big-eyed deer

riding banana-seat bikes
around the cul-de-sac, wheels spinning
through drifts of crunchy leaves
and mothers worried that we would lose
our scarves, hats
and innocence

eyes not big enough
to contain so many colors
the chill that would bite
our cheeks red, make us wear thermals
under dime store Halloween costumes

elusive stars of milkweed
blown across neighbors' yards
helicopter trees, seed pods we would gather,
toss up in the air by handfuls
and watch fall, whirring around us

rolling down browning hills
the world turning over faster
than our stomachs would turn,
crazy laughter spiraling behind us
Chinese jump rope and cat's cradle
leaning against the warm brick buildings
of school, letting the recess sun
warm friendships and faces

today autumn is theoretical,
isolated to specific trees
a lone maple flaming russet
in a neighbor's yard
or something to carry home
in glass globes, buy from postcard racks
back east

calico autumns
and metal lunch boxes
and our mothers calling us in
before the streetlights winked on
before the moths began
to beat against the screen doors,
begging for warmth

Oreos, Part 2

One of the worst insults
is to be called *Oreo*:

Brown on the outside, White on the inside.

People get called *coconut*, too.
That seems more appropriate for me
since coconuts grow in Sri Lanka,
but equally affronting.

I don't worry
about becoming an Oreo.
No one lets me forget my brownness.
Ever.

A Friendly Ghost

I find my costume at Tip-Top Stationers,
smiling mask gazing up at me
through the cellophane window. I hug the box
to my chest, carry it to the register.
On the car ride home, Casper rests
on the seat next to me,
promises the best candy haul ever.

On the night of Halloween, I climb
into a new self. Nylon skin whispers
against my corduroy pants and turtleneck,
envelops me in phantasm. I fit his face
over mine, try on whiteness for the first time.
I feel the power of invisibility, blend
into the river of trick-or-treaters,
at last anonymous.

This year, I don't beg
for candy. I ring doorbells,
plant my sneakers on every porch,
demand the sweetness due me.

Malli learns to walk, suddenly

on the first Halloween after we move
to 2 Revere Place. He is a timid baby,
crawls everywhere at fifteen-months-old.
He pulls himself to standing, circumnavigates rooms
clings to furniture, wainscoting, and
Ammi's legs.

When *Ammi* answers the front door
to the first group of costumed neighborhood kids
the shouts of *Trick or Treat* startle *Malli*
to his tiny feet, send him sprinting to safety.

How could we know those first steps
would lengthen to the cadence of an athlete,
long legs striding the breadth of the world,
fearing nothing?

Youth in Asia

In 1972, the U.S. Senate holds
the first national hearings on
youth in Asia, something about
dignity and human rights.
All the Asian kids I know live
in the tri-state area, so this debate is
beyond my apprehension.

One October we are each given
a tin can with a slot cut in the top
for coins. Our teachers tell us to carry
our cans with us trick-or-treating,
collect money for UNICEF
to help children in other countries.
The cans have photos on them that look like
me. I gather nickels and dimes
for poor kids in Bangladesh and Cambodia
living all in tents
and purposes.

As I grow up news stories of civil wars
and refugee camps euthanize
my naivety, put to sleep
the milk can faces
by nickels and dimes.

Easter Sunday 2019
a series of bomb blasts shatters
an island in the Indian sea, killing
UNICEF kids
with my face.

Good-bye, youth in Asia.

But in this paper view world
they fade into Bolivians,
one brown face as good as another.
I illiterate them from memory.

School Uniform

When I am in the fourth grade
I convince *Ammi* to buy me
a New York Yankees jacket.
It becomes my uniform. Sporting it
around the schoolyard authenticates me
as a native-born New Yorker.
I wear it every day the year after
the Bronx Bombers take the pennant,
its pockets stuffed with baseball cards
and stale chewing gum.

I don't know this is the last year
we will live in New York,
don't know I will have to exchange
navy blue poplin for a satin skating jacket,
molt my skin, start the process again.

V.

Preschool Playhouse Birthday

Ammi and *Thaaththi* bring
Carvel Ice Cream cups
and a Little Golden Book
for each classmate, my name
inscribed in every cover

kids leave off collecting
inch worms in Dixie cups,
abandon the swing set,
resume seats at long, low tables
to sing me "Happy Birthday"

spoon childhood into hungry mouths
clasp fairy tales in eager hands

Cold Turkey

For my sixth birthday,
I receive one gift:
a father who gives up
cigarettes.

This is what I know of love.

One birthday I receive a toy microscope,

my favorite gift. I carry it around
in a tin Disney World lunchbox. Included is
a collection of prepared slides—
mosquitos, onion cells and honeybee wings—
minature worlds tucked where a baloney sandwich
and Hostess cupcake should go. There's a stash
of blank slides clicking in a white cardboard box,
alongside stoppered bottles of fixative and dye.

Ammi and *Thaaththi* help me prepare new slides:
teeming drops of puddle water, cheek cell scrapings
stained with methylene blue, eyelashes peering
from beneath glass cover slips. My physician parents see
themselves in my small body bent over the scope.

Thaaththi teaches me to make a blood smear.
He pricks my finger with a lancet, shows me
how to take a droplet and glide it across slick glass
in a thin carmine haze. I clip the slide to the stage,
peer into the eyepiece. In the field of cells,
hundreds of tiny red saucers,
I search for myself.

An Unknown Religion

In the Raines's kitchen,
Pam's mom grates potatoes
for latkes, deposits the shavings
in a glass bowl filled with water.
Pam and I drink Hi-C from plastic tumblers
while Mrs. Raines preps for the night's meal
and talks to us about the eight nights
of Hannukah, the miracle of light.
I look out the window, watch their neighbors
begin to string colored bulbs along the roof line,
red and green winking on in the twilight.

Mrs. Raines asks about my holiday plans,
wants to know if we attend midnight mass
as a family, do we put up a Christmas tree.
She will not understand how we make
puja on January first, burn linen wicks
in a brass oil lamp, eat *kiri bath* for good luck.
I tell her we belong to a religion
that she has probably never heard of,
since no one in our town
belongs to our temple. She asks me
the name of our religion, and when I tell her
Buddhism she laughs at my definition
of obscure.

But everyone I know at school
is either Catholic or Jewish,
excused early once a week
for catechism classes or Hebrew school.
Being Buddhist is a lonely island
in a sea of electric menorahs
and plastic lawn nativities,
Baby Jesus glowing in His manger
every night of December.

Oh! Tannenbaum!

My Buddhist parents recently moved
to a new house in the suburbs
make a trip to the Nanuet Mall
on Christmas Eve,

dismantle the floor model at store closing,
pack corn husk dolls, strings of lights,
and glass ornaments back into boxes
while the store clerk watches, arms crossed,

so that *Nangi, Malli* and I
in footed pajamas
wake up to a new, bigger tree
on Christmas morning,

a tree to rival any
on this new street, in this new town,
the twinkling bulbs bright enough
for Santa to see from a neighbor's rooftop.

Slumber, Parties

Ammi and *Thaaththi* pack an overnight bag
when we go to holiday parties in other towns.
After the dessert dishes are cleared away,
Nangi, *Malli* and I change out of our party clothes
into matching footed pajamas
before we are bundled into the car
for the drive back to Tappan.

After he pulls into the garage,
Thaaththi carries our sleeping bodies upstairs
one by one, deposits us into our beds.
He lives each day delivering children
into a wide-awake world full of hidden dangers.
But during these holiday nights,
he lets us dream, unaware of icy roads,
buffered from the flurry outside.

Ceylonese Christmas

those Christmas parties
at 2 Revere Place, after we moved
out of the Bronx and into the suburbs,
when *Thaaththi* learned to salt
the driveway with the first snows, bought
shovels to clear the path to the front door

thrown open a dozen times a night, every time
with the questions *"Kohomada? Oyā kalada innē?"*
"How are you? Have you eaten yet?"
followed by embraces, coats heaped
on the king bed in my parents' room, bottles of gifted scotch
deposited on the bar, presents in shiny paper
placed under a tinseled tree, ornaments hung
as high as child arms could reach

when everyone spoke English
with more British idiom than American
before we were Sinhala, Tamil, Burgher
and Muslim, before a civil war
our parents left behind, before Sri Lankan
when we were all Ceylonese

whisper of silk and crepe-de-chine saris
tinkle of armloads of gold bangles
polyester slacks and batik shirts over turtlenecks
adults circulate, laughter and conversation over

low hum of the hi-fi, Christmas music on LP
followed later with the *Saturday Night Fever* soundtrack
and, later still, *baila* records and dancing
in the finished basement, lights dimmed low
the clinking of ice in plastic tumblers full
of Johnny Walker Red for uncles,
Canada Dry Ginger Ale for aunties who

congregated in the kitchen
to refill platters of hors d'oeuvres,
fish cutlets and shrimp *vadai* along side
Chung King brand egg rolls
and cubes of ham and Velveeta skewered
on frilled party picks, sometimes topped
with a chunk of canned pineapple,
sometimes a Maraschino cherry,

foil pans of rice studded with raisins and cloves
Pyrex casserole dishes of pork curry and *brinjal*
dhal kept warm in the oven, bags of *pappadams*
in oil-stained brown paper grocery bags

and me and my siblings and play-cousins,
dressed in our corduroy pants and sweaters
maxi dresses, knee socks and patent-leather Mary Janes
hair tied back with grosgrain ribbons,
how we practiced singing
Jingle Bells and *Silent Night*, twinkle lights
reflected on the foil wrapping paper
and in our eyes, how we practiced holiday rites
we learned at school, practiced feeling
just as American as every other house on Revere Place

our tree framed in the front window
snow falling in large flakes outside,
covering the world in white

VI.

Ammi Cuts Her Hair, or My First Brush with Women's Liberation

Ammi cuts her waist-length hair
into a pageboy, more practical
for her life as a young mother, easier
to style for her days at the hospital.
For *Nangi*, *Malli*, and me, she is
one of Charlie's Angels,
only prettier.

At a party at Uncle Jay's house,
men are aghast when they see her shorn locks.
How could you let your wife cut
her long hair? they ask *Thaaththi*.
He smiles and shrugs, says

Well, it is on her head.

When we are big

I sit at *Ammi's* dressing table
as she prepares to go out. I watch her
straighten the pleats of her sari,
touch up her makeup,
apply L'Air du Temps
to pulse points. I tell her

When we are big
we will put on
lipstick and high heels
and go to parties
with our husbands.

And that is exactly what we did.

Pierced Ears

Thaaththi borrows an earring gun
from the hospital. *Nangi* and I take turns
sitting on a kitchen chair, waiting. He numbs
our earlobes with rubbing alcohol, counts down
from 3, sudden lightning strike of the gun
our first lesson in the pain of beauty.

Suddenly we are initiated into a new realm
of pretty. Sri Lankan aunties will gift us
tiny gold flowers, twenty-two karat stars
to ornament our budding femininity. We want
to cut our hair short, make sure everyone knows
how grown up we are now.

Death Comes to Revere Place

Jesse Ennison loves to watch the cars
drive past our street, waves
from his place on the swing set.
He is bigger than the rest of us,
but is gentle with the littler kids.

Mrs. Ennison says Jesse is special.
Ammi and *Thaaththi* say he has something
called Down Syndrome. We shrug,
fold him into our games,
part of the neighborhood pack.

Sometimes I go to the Ennison's
to play with his sister Shari.
Jesse gives up his swing
for me. He pushes me higher, laughs
when I squeal with pretend fear.

The year after Jesse's bar mitzvah
an ambulance wails
up the Ennison's driveway.
It's Easter Sunday, so everyone
on the cul-de-sac is home.

Neighbors appeal to *Ammi* and *Thaaathti*,
the two doctors on our block, to do
something. Ask the right questions
of the ambulance driver.
Somehow help.

But it is too late for Jesse, his big heart
too much for this world.
He is the first person I know
who died,

a kid, like me.

Party Dressed

Nangi and I wear matching frocks
hand-made by our *Aachchi*.
Gingham checks in red and blue
for the bicentennial, edged in rick-rack.
Pink-striped maxi dresses with ruffled cuffs
and deep flounced hems. Velvet mini-dresses
in hydrangea shades with long belled sleeves.

She creates our dresses in her mind's eye,
without tissue paper patterns bought
from House of Fabrics. She glides scissors
through yards of flowers, imagines us petaled.
She smiles around straight pins pursed
between her lips, tells us to stand still
while she adjusts cloth against our squirming bodies.
Her glinting needle leaves miles of gathers in its wake.

When our friends' parents ask us
Where'd your mom find such pretty clothes?
we smile and shrug, smooth our skirts
with the palms of our small hands, say

Oh, you can't buy these in a store—
our Aachchi made them

before we skip back to a childhood
petticoated in eyelet,
yoked in lace, gift-wrapped
in wide satin sashes.

Flight Paths, or How Tall Is a Bag of Basmati Rice

The door to the pantry is painted white,
brush marks mimicking woodgrain,
the occasional hair from the brush embedded
in the surface like a whisker or a bristle of foxtail
carried in from the schoolyard on the arm
of a coat. Along the door jamb are pencil marks,
temperatures etched on a thermometer.
Each mark bears a name and an age.
Manik, age three, Ashini, age four,
Aruni, age six. The marks start
near the lower shelves where rice
is stored in twenty-pound zippered sacks,
so many slouching pillowcases. Each year we inch
upwards, past the Froot Loops
and Kraft Macaroni and Cheese, past
glass bottles of Taster's Choice and Nescafé
now filled with roasted curry powder,
turmeric, and pale green cardamom pods.
Hash marks race to the top of the doorway,
charting our flights.

What I Like Best About Ballet Class Is the Uniformity

I carry my dance clothes in a vinyl ballet box
decorated with pictures of girls in tutus and pointe shoes.
At the Dodge Dance Studio, *Ammi* helps me change
into pale tights, black nylon leotard and slippers
the color of a first kiss.

We take our places at the barre, our starfish hands
carving space with *port de bras*. Our toes draw
wobbly *rond de jambe* circles on the floor. We practice
off-tempo to Puccini, the record player
hissing and popping in the corner.

The wooden floor is marked with black tape
asterisks. Each of us stands on a star,
mimics the five ballet positions our teacher demonstrates.
Like the crabapple tree in the yard at home, she is
suspended spring, a riot of blooming.

I crave the anonymity of identical tights and leotards,
the three rows of little girls on asterisks,
small feet forming matching v's against wood grain,
no one conspicuous, no one foreign.

Bouquets

At the end of the school year,
Ammi cuts one bloom off each
of fifty-seven rosebushes to make bouquets
for our elementary school teachers.
She snaps the thorns off each stem,
wraps half-open buds in pink crepe paper.

I follow her around the yard, read words
like *Double Delight*, *Yankee Doodle*,
Sterling and *Cherish* embossed on green tin tags
at the base of each rosebush, dream
of a career naming flowers.

Baptism

I am seven years old the first time someone erases me.

She is also seven, all curly hair and bravado.
She corners me in the back yard
at Shari Ennison's birthday,
gives my party dress with pink satin sash
a withering look, asks

What are you, anyway?

as though I am a new species of bug
she wants to trap in an empty jam jar.

I am confused by her question, think
I'm a girl, like you. We go to the same school.

She rolls her eyes, says

No, I mean what ARE you—
where are you FROM?

I want to say *I live across the street*
but I don't. I tell her that I am Ceylonese,
that my parents are from a place far away
but I am from here. She narrows her eyes.

I have never heard of that.
You're making it up.

I think about the framed batiks on our walls,
the brass oil lamps lit at Vesak,
Aachchi grinding split peas for *vadai*,
the aunties, uncles and play cousins
who make up our sphere.

I start to question the existence of it all.

She pulls me to the above ground pool,
forces me up the ladder with her. We stare
into the water, study our undulating faces.

You're Black, she hisses, *but you don't want
anyone to know, so you made up something else.*

She spits the word at me, a threat,
something to deny.

She rolls a single syllable in her mouth,
feels the power of naming her world,
teaches me a lifelong ritual
of being defined by other mouths.

She shoves me towards my reflection
until I tumble into the water.

I walk home dripping pool across Revere Place,
my pink sash dragging behind me.

A New Species

Mrs. Carpenter is 1970s pretty,
feathered hair, thin and athletic. She wears
bell-bottomed jeans with matching vests,
hoop earrings and platform sandals. She laughs
easy and long, eyes crinkling at the corners.
She never makes us feel bad for asking
questions, encourages our inquisitive minds. I think
of her as a cool aunt I wish would come over
for Thanksgiving. Everyone in the second grade
has a crush on Mrs. Carpenter.

She shows us how to grow beans in Dixie cups,
explains what makes the roots extend down
and the shoots reach skyward. She hooks us on phonics,
sorts us into color-coded reading groups, gives us
new multiplication tables to memorize. She giggles
when she recites *my very eager mother*
just served us nine pickles to help us order planets
of the solar system. She conjures recycled paper
from news pulp, pages fragile as doilies.

Mrs. Carpenter is married to a marine biologist
who spends weeks on a boat looking
for new species of coral. She tells our class
that he has been to Sri Lanka, an island
in the Indian Ocean, smiles at me
when she points to a teardrop in the blue
of the world map. She shows us her ring
set with a dark sapphire. My classmates, skeptical,
say I'm really from somewhere else,
somewhere they have heard of.

They haven't seen our house draped
with batiks depicting the *Perahara*, haven't held
elephant statues carved of teak and jackfruit wood,
haven't heard the tinkling of leaf-shaped pendants
on our brass oil lamp at home. I have learned
not to argue with them when they re-write
my history.

One day Mr. Carpenter surprises us.
I recognize him from the framed picture
on her desk. Mrs. Carpenter laughs,
hugs her husband in front of the whole class.
She makes a point to introduce me, announces
I am from the place he found her wedding ring.

He says *ayubowan* to me, palms pressed together,
teaches the class this means *may you have a long life*.
He tells us the sea in Sri Lanka is a rainbow of fish.

My classmates steal looks at the map,
imagine coconut palms and temples,
start to believe I am real.

Saplings

after Ann Brantingham's Dogwood Leaf

Ammi and *Thaaththi* plant
two dogwoods and a Japanese maple
in the front yard of 2 Revere Place,
a tree for each of us. There is a pink
dogwood for *Nangi* and a red one
for me. The maple is for *Malli*. We name
the dogwoods Pinky and Rudy.
I can't remember what we name
the maple.

We encircle them with brick,
protect them from weeds, each tree
in a small suburban fort. We water
each sapling with the long garden hose.
In the afternoons *Nangi*, *Malli* and I sit
on the grass, cool and green,
next to our trees. We read to them,
select the most encouraging words
from our library books.

When we move away from 2 Revere Place,
we whisper our goodbyes to Pinky, Rudy
and *Malli's* maple. We watch them nodding
in the yard as the car pulls away. We hope
the new family remembers to tell stories
to our trees. We hope they root
as well as we did.

Ars Poetica

Mr. Fialko teaches us
simile and metaphor
one pale spring afternoon
in Language Arts class.

She is as fit as a fiddle,
he is gentle as a lamb
he jots on the chalkboard.
Her smile is a butterfly,
the sun is a ripe orange.

Every afternoon we craft
our own comparisons,
transmute our suburban lives
into something less prosaic.
We turn in our revised worlds,
and he publishes our work
on the school mimeograph machine,
the drum humming, coughing out
lavender lines.

I leave the fourth-grade chasing
words like feathers
to the cliff's edge, just beyond
my reach. I hurl myself seaward,
plummeting like a stone, until
an updraft of poetry catches
me, fills my newly-fledged wings.

VII.

Cold Comfort Food

I scour the internet, looking
for the recipe closest to *Ammi's*,
then grab my car keys
for a trip to Walmart.
I push my cart with a wobbly wheel
up and down the aisles, searching
for names: Kraft, Chicken of the Sea,
Veg-All and Ritz. I collect ingredients
while the calendar pages
flutter.

At home in the kitchen I read
the blue and orange box, feel
the weight of prepare-as-directed.
Open cans, toss the jagged lids
carelessly in the bin. Measure milk, cut butter
into neat pats, flake tuna into pink splinters.
Swirl together in a heavy-bottomed pot, then spill
into a greased Pyrex dish. Sand the top
with cracker crumbs. I stare
in the little oven door window
and wait.

Today the whole house
smells like 1974. I serve a portion
(always an edge piece, where the noodles
are brownest), and every forkful fills me
with a Formica-countered childhood. I swallow
innocence. I swallow ignorance
of how my mother prepared us meals
like tuna casserole and Hamburger Helper
instead of *parippu* and *kukul mas* curry. I swallow years
of my family feeding ourselves on
America, the country that decades later spits us out,
desperate to rinse the taste of immigrants
from its snarling mouth.

The next day I pull the dish
from the refrigerator, peel back the foil.
I stand barefoot on the tile floor, eat
directly from the pan, not bothering
to heat leftovers. Every bite sticks
in my throat, congealed. I choke
each mouthful down. I can't
bring myself to waste
memory.

Unbeautiful

no cornflower-blue eyes
instead
burning embers
more suited to kohl than mascara
brows arched in perpetual surprise

no golden hair that feathers
perfectly à la Farrah Fawcett
repeatedly tucks the same loose strand
behind her right ear

Maybelline ads are wasted here.

She's not beautiful.
self-conscious about the gap in her front teeth
maybe she smiles anyway

no endless supply of
Fair and Lovely Lightening Cream
will fade
cinnamon skin,
bark of some other rare tree

dip of waist flaring to
fecund curves
prized in the tropics,
not here in this
City of Angels

No two-inch thigh gap here.

speaks quietly, sotto voce
lean in to catch every word
pronounced lisp at once child-like and sexy
sudden laugh loud as a stack of plates breaking

She is no classic beauty,
yet haunting
in her every imperfection.

The world drab without her,
this unbeautiful girl.

When Brown Bodies Make the News

they are extras in a Duran Duran music video,
natives included in the shoot to lend local color.
This faraway place enters our collective consciousness
and we muse about going there someday
to loll on white beaches while sarong-d boys
bring us drinks decorated with hibiscus flowers.

When brown bodies make the news
our eyes flit over stories of civil wars
and suicide bombers. We can't believe
the kinds of atrocities that happen
over there, far away from sanitized studios
where we practice yoga. We press our palms
together in co-opted *namaste*, roll up our mats,
feel somehow enlightened.

When brown bodies make the news
we think how sad it is to see so many bodies
washed up on such beautiful beaches. We Google
"how to know if a tsunami is coming"
and learn to seek higher ground,
unlike those poor local fishermen, their huts flattened,
their children devoured by the sea. We surf
past these grim images in search of uplifting stories
of tourists who survive the wave and return
home to whole, dry houses.

When brown bodies make the news
they are pawns in tragedy, studded with shrapnel.
They are anonymous, not related to parents
or cousins or communities. We pause
to read news stories because the tragedy
is on Easter Sunday, a pastel day. We scan
the reports and count how many Americans
and Europeans are affected, consume details
about how lucky these pale bodies are to escape
disaster, how much those who are lost will be missed.

When brown bodies make the news, we are
just bodies. There are plenty more
where we came from. Tomorrow's news
will wash us away. Water sluices
across a scarred church, rinses away
the blood, the vivid of red against brown diluted.

Kitchen Counter

the makeshift operating table
when *Thaaththi* stitches us
back together after we fall
off our bikes or get scuffed
playing kickball on cul-de-sac,

my first writing desk
where every summer
I write stories, pencil lines wobbly,
homework assigned by *Aachchi*
where I must use ten new words,
epics I must complete
before I can go outside to play,

where I drink strawberry Quik
and watch *Ammi* prepare
Hamburger Helper lasagna,
the dinners we beg her to make,
meals that will make us
an American family

and not *those immigrants*
who moved into 2 Revere Place.

Cardamom Vowels

Your name is not
an apology, the sound kowtowing
to ears accustomed to Jennifers
and Debbies. You are a namesake
for a temple rising
in the Chao Phraya River,
face to the morning sun. Your name
is mantra, meant for repetition.

Your name is not
a question, voice rising at the end.
Unlearn the habit
of asking. Hold the magic
of Sanskrit in your throat.
Orient yourself with definitions:
red dawns, lotus offerings,
the padding steps of lions' feet
in forests of rare trees,
groves that tremble incantation.

Your name is not
a punchline. You are not obliged
to accept awkward nicknames
and laugh, not required
to contort your tongue
into a foreign shape. Don't grow towards
mispronunciation, dividing yourself
into two people. Remove ill-fitting shoes
that chafe along the seams; roam
barefoot in the halls of your name.

Unlearn a lifetime
of answering to
not your name. Make them taste
your name, their unknowing tongues
prickling with tamarind.
Shape their mouths around
cardamom vowels,
your syllables turmeric. Teach them
to whisper spice, intone fire.

Eating at Home
for Ammi, who feeds me

My definition of home
is the house where my family lives,
where I am still young
and depend on the group
to define who I am
in the wide world. Home is
where my name comes
natural as words
like *safe* and *sky*,
school and *blue* and *dinner*.
Home is the roundness of vowels,
names that tie me to an island lush
with groves of cinnamon,
breadfruit, coconut palms.
Home is sunlight I can drink,
warmth of cardamom,
floral and familiar,
coriander and cumin
like dust and smoke and ash.

Home is plates of rice and dhal,
taste of curries and gravies
dyed sienna with roasted curry powder,
afternoon yellow of turmeric,
and my *Ammi's* voice asking
if I want more okra, more chutney.
Home is aroma that lingers
on my fingertips only here
where I am secure enough
to eat with my fingers, sink
into the sensory experience
of truly eating,
the tactile joys of rice and curry,
where I am not estranged from my meals
with fork and spoon.

These meals I will learn
to replicate in my own kitchen,
following notes written
in *Ammi's* tidy hand,
recipe instructions incomprehensible
with measurements of palm-ful and dash,
except I have witnessed her prepare
a procession of these meals over my lifetime
at home.

In the slanting light
seeping in through half-closed blinds
we drink tea
(not like the English)
sweetened with teaspoons of condensed milk,
the names Borden or Carnation peeping
out of the cupboard above the electric teapot,
next to Tupperware containers
of loose-leaf tea from Champika's estate,
or if we are feeling lazy, tea bags
(never Lipton's)
flutter of tags marked Dilmah
we buy across town
in Artesia from the few shelves
at Pioneer Cash and Carry
that stock the groceries and brands
we use to make meals
at home.

Weeds

n. a valueless plant growing wild, especially one that grows on cultivated ground to the exclusion or injury of the desired crop.

—dictionary.com

What is a weed? A plant whose virtues have not yet been discovered.

—Ralph Waldo Emerson

kids from immigrant families
grow like weeds
refuse to be uprooted
thrive amongst local flora
spark bright spots in the lawn
inextinguishable yellow
assert themselves to gardeners
who would pluck them early
for their audacious blooming

To My Seven-Year-Old Self

1. Teachers will try to give you a new name, easier, more American. Annie, Amy, Ruthie or Ruby. Their pencils will struggle to form the letters of your name on roll sheets, vowels in new places, consonants unexpectedly soft. Insist on the name that is your legacy.

2. Neighbors will tell you that you are not American. They will refer to your home as the corner house the immigrant family moved into. This will stay with you all of your American life, from your birth in New York City to every adult interaction with grocery store cashiers.

3. Kids at school will tell you Sri Lanka isn't a real place because they have never heard of it, insist you have invented a country. Unfurl maps, spin the globe, spell out the letters of Lanka in a steady hand.

4. Big people will tease you for being short. They have forgotten the power of smallness.

5. People will tell you that boys are mean because they like you, justify the shoving and teasing and pulling of ponytails. Remember gentleness is something you deserve.

6. Adults will tell you not to be so shy. They will brush the hair from your eyes, nudge you to the front, ask you to play the piano at family parties. Build a room of quiet in your heart, retreat when the clamor of the world is too loud. Embrace the stillness of you.

7. Well-intentioned speech therapists will try to correct your lisp, assign exercises to unravel your tongue. They will be uncomfortable with the sound. Know your words need no correction.

    Your voice is meant to be heard.

Thaaththi **always carries a handkerchief**

folded in his pants pocket. On Father's Day
we go to Bamburger's looking
for handkerchiefs. Three to a box,
each embroidered with his initial,
one blue, one red, and one tan,
shingled beneath the clear plastic lid.

Thaaththi, always ready
with his hanky, tells us
to blow our noses. He dips
the corners into water glasses
at Szechwan Gardens, wipes duck sauce
from the corners of our mouths.
We bark our shins on the asphalt
of Revere Place
and he cleans up our cuts,
dries our tears, sends us
back into the world.

Thaaththi carries the weight of childhood
neatly folded in the creases of wash-soft linen.

Guavas

winter sun goldens guavas
though we eat them green
crisp and grainy with salt

tree sprouted from pearls
rescued from the pulp, dried
between layers of paper towels

because *Aachchi* could foster
any seed, coax groves
from the most reluctant pips

fruit bursts possibility
our chins dripping sweet
deep into December

Thread

Aachchi sends
two strands of thread
in a small white envelope
with a note

Dearest Aruni,

> *Herewith pirith nool*
for you and Jeff.

Hope everything is OK with you.
May the Thisarana bless you both
with health, happiness and
success always.

> *Love always,*
> *Aachchi*

trusts the USPS to deliver
blessings of Lord Buddha, hopes
a thirty-seven-cent stamp
will buy passage for miracles
to encircle our wrists

How to make savory rice (according to *Ammi*)

Ingredients

half a medium onion, finely chopped
      allow time for tears to well
      spill down your cheeks, splash
      on the bamboo cutting board

two to three tablespoons ghee
      scooped from a glass jar
      your reflection pools, shimmers
      in the belly of a hot skillet

five to six green cardamom pods
      cradle in the bowl of your hand
      let floral seep into skin
      allow them to drop gently
      into a mortar to bruise

one tablespoon salt
      don't measure with a spoon
      learn to feel weight of the sea
      in cupped palm

two sprigs of *karapincha*
      tender leaves plucked from the back yard
      or if the tree is still too young to harvest
      buy from Pioneer Cash and Carry
      (it won't be out with the other vegetables—
      ask the young cashier to sell you a dollar bag
      from stash under the register)

one-and-a-half-inch piece cinnamon stick
      broken slightly, splinters the color of you
      and of men peeling fragrant bark
      from deep groves half a world away
      rolling cigars of warm wood

fifteen to twenty whole cloves
        tiny buds to spark small fires
        on the tongue—
        remember flowers
        contain their own power

fifteen to twenty whole black peppercorns
        harvested from a spice garden,
        red pearls plucked, boiled black
        dried under a hot island sun

three cups Basmati rice
        each grain holds the green
        of paddy fields, strength
        of shoots pushing skyward, weight
        of the bent sheaf

one teaspoon turmeric
        yellow to tint fingertips gold
        stain mouths with the language
        of fire, history of Kandyan kings

water, or chicken stock,
        bubbling aromatic in the rice cooker
        scent the kitchen with welcome

a handful of sultanas
        sweeten the pot by mouthful
        raisins plump in steam, regain
        memory of vine

Spending Yom Kippur with Waylon Jennings

The hillsides now dotted by tract homes
were once oil fields,
derricks like steel birds bowing
on the shale hills of La Mirada.
At the Beach Boulevard Arco station,
forty dollars buys me
partial passage across the desert.

I join the river of cars
snaking the Inland Empire,
weathered pickups, silver Hondas,
semis with silhouettes on mud flaps
and growling Harleys.

California sweeps backward down the highway,
desert miles sheeting off my car,
skipping like loose gravel. I speed
past windmill fields
and decapitated palms trees.
As I cross the state line
the Colorado slips by, awash in reeds.
I could cast my sins into the water.

Ragged mountains tumble
across the sand, slouching eastward.
The sun sets in my side mirrors,
a giant, yawning maw
consuming California behind me,
propelling me through the night
toward Phoenix.

Yom Kippur dawns monsoonal.
On Highway 17, I listen to
The Essential Waylon Jennings,
and he is cantor for the drive,
revealing secrets and ancient truths.

The Mesa Cemetery across from
the Oakland A's spring training camp
is landscaped with juniper, orange and olive trees.
I search the plots, anticipating
a large stone marker littered
with gifts and mementos,
an altar to the Outlaw.

My mind travels back
to the mid-1970s, riding shotgun
in a sunset orange AMC Hornet,
country music drifting out of the AM radio.
I think about my mother, a recent transplant
from Sri Lanka, traversing Rockland County
with Waylon's words flooding the car,
how she used these tales of love
gone wrong, heartache and longing to decode
a new culture. Did she pity
good-hearted women
in love with good-timing men?
Did she yearn for life in Luckenbach?
What 1970s immigrant was not deserving
of the Wurlitzer Prize, refusing
to get over someone left behind?
These days in the passenger seat,
listening to my mom sing along
to Waylon, told me what it means
to be American.

His grave is marked by
a black marble slab;
the only allowance for individuality
is a laser-etched portrait
and the flying "W" logo.
All plots here are decorated
with silk flowers and flags.
A single, wilted red rose
is tucked between the flowers.
A handwritten note reads
Janet Monk Glass said to say hi.
He is surrounded by
World War II vets, children,

Freemasons, Slavs, Croats, and Mormons.
Waylon was an average guy,
an unmet poet who helped us navigate
the heartbreak of life.

I brush dried grass from his portrait.
On this day of atonement,
I think about the Outlaw, wonder
if he felt a need for absolution.
Did he feel a misplaced guilt
for the plane crash, haunted by the ghost
of Buddy Holly? Survivor's obsession
with success resonates
with all immigrants, casualties
of sacrifice and distance.

On this holiest of days, I pray
Waylon forgave himself.
Neither of us are Jewish, but I pray
for renewal in the year ahead.
Warm rain falls on us both,
washing away failures,
cleansing us for the new cycle.
I find a stone to lay on the marker
to bear witness to my visit.
I join a part of my soul with his,
my mitzvah.

What We Found in Uncle's House

twin boys in matching blue playsuits
captured at Sears Portrait Studio,
the plastic frame cracked
but free from dust

a globe with the old borders,
naming dead centuries, defunct empires
Baltic states swallowed
inside the USSR

one hundred and forty dollars' worth
of US postage stamps,
letters unsent, surplus of empty envelopes
yawning in their carton

three electric rice cookers
of varying cup capacity
steaming basmati rice for one

two hundred and seventeen bottles of vitamins
supplements for heart health, brain health
and virility, fistfuls
of immortality

four blue tins of Danish butter cookies,
cellophane wrappers intact

thirty-one caps balanced
on a wooden hat rack,
a tree of tweed nests
emptied of birds

three sets of bangles, sized for future
daughters-in-law,
six bangles per set,
green, orange and turquoise, studded
with brass,
price tags fluttering
one hundred and seventy-five rupees

a plastic box containing
forty-three paper clips and
Auntie's wedding ring
set with cloudy diamonds
and a single pearl

seven copies of the Quran,
one illuminated in gold calligraphy
one held together with duct tape
one small enough to tuck into a sedan glovebox

a .22-caliber rifle, not loaded

a maroon prayer rug
layered atop a foam pad,
facing Mecca

and fifteen packets of seeds
brought back from Hyderabad
brinjal
bitter gourd
green chili
lady's finger—

never planted, no unruly vines
overrunning garden borders
the way sons cannot be
contained

The Things Left

you think that you left things
behind, forgotten in the coat closet
at 2 Revere Place, tucked in the back
behind the winter coats and ice skates,
or left behind

in the garage, leaning against the wall
closest to *Ammi's* orange AMC Hornet,
the one with AM radio only, songs that
drifted out the speakers, songs from the *Grease*
soundtrack, "Hopelessly Devoted to You" and
"You're the One That I Want," acting out
scenes from the movie, the neighborhood kids
taking turns at Danny and Sandy and Rizzo,
or those other songs

left in the cabinet
of the big black console stereo crouching
in the basement, echoes of
the *Saturday Night Fever* soundtrack
electric-sliding up the stairs and

into the kitchen where *Thaaththi* is blowing up
more balloons that he rubs against his curly hair
to generate the static that sticks them to the wall
and on Monday morning there will still be
crepe paper streamers left

Scotch-taped to the wood paneling, still
crumpled wrapping paper left
on the floor, exposed gifts of Monopoly
and Connect Four piled on a folding table and left-

over birthday cake sweating sugar
onto a Pyrex dish in the kitchen fridge,
the pink roses bleeding
into the white frosting, ballerina candles blown
out, tilting arabesques next to your icing name, left

waiting for you to eat,
like you eat the dogwood trees, pink and red
in the front yard of 2 Revere Place, eat
the Toughskin jeans, stiff and impossibly indigo, eat
the purple banana-seat bike whizzing
down Howard Avenue, eat the 17-year cicadas
and the baseball cards
and the last half-ounce of *Ammi's* Bluegrass eau de toilette,

you've eaten all these things
because we grew up in a home
where nothing ever goes to waste,
nothing left behind on the plate

Their days were measured

in miles between
the Married Officers' Quarters
on the air force base in China Bay
and the beach at Trinco where men hauled in
the day's catch at sunset. Small silver flames
arching in the nets. The errant stingray
returned to the sea.

Days measured from the day they left
for the Katunayake Airport. Whole family
waving from the tarmac. December thirty-first
flight, British Overseas Airways Corporation plane,
the turning of a new year, new leaf,

or the hours of that first leg to Amsterdam,
the flower fields asleep under a blanket of snow.
Chinese food with friend of a relative, driving
through a slumbering town, boats tucked in
under tarpaulin covers.

Days measured in city blocks.
Steps on the frozen sidewalk
between 1770 Grand Concourse
and the double-doors of Bronx-Lebanon hospital.
Snowflakes the texture of scraped coconut.

Some days in winter were measured
in dollars. Two airline tickets.
The plane trip back to Sri Lanka. Or in meals
of crackers and tinned sardines.

One day was measured
by fundal height. The time between contractions
the Saturday of their first Thanksgiving weekend.

Their days were measured in first smiles. First steps.
First words. First days of school, sandwiches packed
in Snoopy lunchboxes with dimes for milk money,
yellow school buses pulling away from the curb.

Days measured in mortgage payments. First house.
Jackson and Perkins rose bushes, tomatoes on the vine,
the flames of autumn leaves raked into piles.

Days gained momentum, measured pencil marks
charting the flight of three children
in inches on a doorframe.

They learned to seal moments under plastic
on pages of family albums, the Nikon's attempt
to stay the hands of the clock.

About the Author

Aruni Wijesinghe is a project manager, ESL teacher, occasional sous chef and erstwhile belly dance instructor. She holds a BA in English Literature from UCLA, an AA in dance from Cypress College, and a certification in Teaching English to Speakers of Other Languages (TESOL) from UC Irvine.

A Pushcart Prize-nominated poet, her work has been published in journals and anthologies both nationally and internationally. In 2020 she served as guest editor of *Redshift 5*, an anthology of pandemic-themed poetry (Arroyo Seco Press). In 2021 she co-authored *The Undulating Line: Writing Poetry Through Belly Dance* (Picture Show Press), a collection of essays, poems and writing prompts that explores the connection between dance and the poetic impulse. The book *2 Revere Place* is her first solo full-length collection of poetry (Moon Tide Press, May 2022).

She lives a quiet life in Orange County, California with her husband Jeff and their cats Jack and Josie. You can follow her writing at www.aruniwrites.com and on Instagram @aruniwrites.

Acknowledgements

Angels Flight – Literary West: "Cardamom Vowels"

BIPOC Writing Party Anthology: "*Oya kālā dā*"

Cultural Daily: "Glow" and "Goldie Unlocks"

Dryland: A literary journal born in South Central Los Angeles: "If Judy Blume Was My Aunt"

"Lisp" appears in *Can I Sit with You: The Stormy Social Seas of the Schoolyard (Deadwood City Publishing, 2007)*

"Unbeautiful" was first published in *Altadena Poetry Review: Anthology 2019 (Shabda Press, 2019)*

"Eating at Home" appears in *The Bridge: Writings by contemporary writers from Pakistan and the United States, Volume II (The Bridge Volume II, 2020)*

"The Things Left" appears in *Cholla Needles 53 (Cholla Needles, 2021)*

"Banyan" appears in *Words & Images (Sasse Museum of Art, 2022)*

"When Brown Bodies Make the News" is forthcoming in *Beat Not Beat Anthology (Moon Tide Press, 2022)*

With Gratitude

To Eric Morago and the whole team at Moon Tide Press. Thank you for taking a chance on me and this book, and for being so gentle with both of us.

To all my workshop friends. Special shout out to Culturama, BIPOC Writing Party, and Your Poem, Your Voice. It is in these workshops that many of these poems were conceived and refined. Thank you for creating safe spaces and for listening without prejudice. You have made me a better poet and person.

To the open mics and reading series of Los Angeles and Orange Counties for giving me and many writers a place to be heard. Big love to Shout the Open Mic, Two Idiots Peddling Poetry, Future Now, Expressions L.A., Rapp Saloon, Poetry Circus, Library Girl and Roar Shack. Thank you for being the crossroads where I continue to meet some of my dearest friends.

To Ra Avis and Bill Friday, for holding my hand and telling me I contain a story. Thank you for your confidence, encouragement and friendship.

To Robert Fialko, my fourth-grade teacher at William O. Schaefer Elementary in Tappan, New York. Thank you for teaching me the difference between simile and metaphor, the power of words, and the magic of poetry. I'll never forget you.

To David Rocklin, for so many things. I will always maintain that any writing career I might have has a direct line back to you and to Roar Shack, my first literary home. Thank you for being my friend. You define mensch.

To my family. Without you, there is no me.

And to Jeff, my kind, patient husband. Thank you for picking me up and dusting me off when I fall. Thank you for reading countless drafts. Thank you for listening to me quibble over one word or line for hours. Thank you for our life. I love you.

Afterword

so you made up something else
a collage poem by bridgette bianca using words from 2 Revere Place

these pale bodies
desperate for their handful
paint themselves with the glow
of what they destroy
vivid as blood

i have learned not to argue with them
when they re-write
my history
i mark lines
make a blood smear
the vivid of red against brown
i divide myself in two

a sea of electric
folds me in
ripple of teal and emerald
waves
i long to
bridge continents
with fingertips
the burden of the future
rests
against my collarbone
we all hold two countries
suspended from a delicate chain

i have two names
with no one to receive them
i try on words
i bend my tongue
along the seams
on a dark skin of words
count how many
syllables snag
on my teeth
start to believe i am real
demand the sweetness due me

i search for myself
tucked in the back
behind
a god
who doesn't know my name
nothing ever goes to waste
i fit his face over mine
to clear the path
steal a bit of what was stolen

learn to seek higher ground,
sit quietly on the edge of life
before the next leap
see so many bodies
that look like me
stretching
to the horizon

Patrons

Moon Tide Press would like to thank the following people for their support in helping publish the finest poetry from the Southern California region. To sign up as a patron, visit www.moontidepress.com or send an email to publisher@moontidepress.com.

Anonymous
Robin Axworthy
Conner Brenner
Nicole Connolly
Bill Cushing
Susan Davis
Kristen Baum DeBeasi
Peggy Dobreer
Dennis Gowans
Alexis Rhone Fancher
Hanalena Fennel
Half Off Books & Brad T. Cox
Susan Hayden
Donna Hilbert
Jim & Vicky Hoggatt
Michael Kramer
Ron Koertge & Bianca Richards
Gary Jacobelly
Ray & Christi Lacoste
Zachary & Tammy Locklin
Lincoln McElwee
David McIntire
José Enrique Medina
Michael Miller & Rachanee Srisavasdi
Michelle & Robert Miller
Ronny & Richard Morago
Terri Niccum
Andrew November
Jeremy Ra
Luke & Mia Salazar
Jennifer Smith
Andrew Turner
Rex Wilder
Mariano Zaro
Wes Bryan Zwick

Also Available from Moon Tide Press

Here Go the Knives, Kelsey Bryan-Zwick (2022)
Trumpets in the Sky, Jerry Garcia (2022)
Threnody, Donna Hilbert (2022)
A Burning Lake of Paper Suns, Ellen Webre (2021)
Instructions for an Animal Body, Kelly Gray (2021)
Head *V* Heart: New & Selected Poems, Rob Sturma (2021)
Sh!t Men Say to Me: A Poetry Anthology in Response to Toxic Masculinity (2021)
Flower Grand First, Gustavo Hernandez (2021)
Everything is Radiant Between the Hates, Rich Ferguson (2020)
When the Pain Starts: Poetry as Sequential Art, Alan Passman (2020)
This Place Could Be Haunted If I Didn't Believe in Love, Lincoln McElwee (2020)
Impossible Thirst, Kathryn de Lancellotti (2020)
Lullabies for End Times, Jennifer Bradpiece (2020)
Crabgrass World, Robin Axworthy (2020)
Contortionist Tongue, Dania Ayah Alkhouli (2020)
The only thing that makes sense is to grow, Scott Ferry (2020)
Dead Letter Box, Terri Niccum (2019)
Tea and Subtitles: Selected Poems 1999-2019, Michael Miller (2019)
At the Table of the Unknown, Alexandra Umlas (2019)
The Book of Rabbits, Vince Trimboli (2019)
Everything I Write Is a Love Song to the World, David McIntire (2019)
Letters to the Leader, HanaLena Fennel (2019)
Darwin's Garden, Lee Rossi (2019)
Dark Ink: A Poetry Anthology Inspired by Horror (2018)
Drop and Dazzle, Peggy Dobreer (2018)
Junkie Wife, Alexis Rhone Fancher (2018)
The Moon, My Lover, My Mother, & the Dog, Daniel McGinn (2018)
Lullaby of Teeth: An Anthology of Southern California Poetry (2017)
Angels in Seven, Michael Miller (2016)
A Likely Story, Robbi Nester (2014)
Embers on the Stairs, Ruth Bavetta (2014)
The Green of Sunset, John Brantingham (2013)
The Savagery of Bone, Timothy Matthew Perez (2013)
The Silence of Doorways, Sharon Venezio (2013)
Cosmos: An Anthology of Southern California Poetry (2012)
Straws and Shadows, Irena Praitis (2012)
In the Lake of Your Bones, Peggy Dobreer (2012)
I Was Building Up to Something, Susan Davis (2011)

Hopeless Cases, Michael Kramer (2011)
One World, Gail Newman (2011)
What We Ache For, Eric Morago (2010)
Now and Then, Lee Mallory (2009)
Pop Art: An Anthology of Southern California Poetry (2009)
In the Heaven of Never Before, Carine Topal (2008)
A Wild Region, Kate Buckley (2008)
Carving in Bone: An Anthology of Orange County Poetry (2007)
Kindness from a Dark God, Ben Trigg (2007)
A Thin Strand of Lights, Ricki Mandeville (2006)
Sleepyhead Assassins, Mindy Nettifee (2006)
Tide Pools: An Anthology of Orange County Poetry (2006)
Lost American Nights: Lyrics & Poems, Michael Ubaldini (2006)